BORN TO FLY

HUMANS ARE NOT BORN TO CREEP AND TO CRAWL ON EARTH LIKE CATERPILLARS. WE ARE BORN TO TRANSFORM INTO BUTTERFLIES.

by **Bahram Spitama**
and all the wisdom keepers in history.
See the book ABOUT THE AUTHORS

One Printers Way
Altona, MB R0G 0B0
Canada

www.friesenpress.com

Copyright © 2023 by Bahram Spitama
First Edition — 2023

All rights reserved.

No part of this publication may be reproduced in any form, or by any means, electronic or mechanical, including photocopying, recording, or any information browsing, storage, or retrieval system, without permission in writing from FriesenPress.

photo credit to Adobe Stock and Vector Stock

ISBN
978-1-03-918556-2 (Hardcover)
978-1-03-918555-5 (Paperback)
978-1-03-918557-9 (eBook)

1. RELIGION, ZOROASTRIANISM

Distributed to the trade by The Ingram Book Company

Table of Contents

About The Authors		ix
Acknowledgements		xiii
Glossary		xvii
Introduction		1
	An Unconscious Existence	1
	Our World Needs Wisdom	4
	The Truth Will Set You Free, but it Will Hurt	8
	Tell Me the Truth, but Don't Tell Me the Truth	9
	Intention	10
Chapter 1	**Zarathustra**	13
	The Wise Zarathustra	13
	Ahura Mazda: The Union of Consciousness and Wisdom	21
	The God Within	24
	The Twin Spirits: Unity, Not Duality	25
	Ahriman (Evil)	26
	Hell and Heaven	26
Chapter 2	**Free to Choose**	28
	The Choice Is Yours	28
	Two Sides of a Coin	29
	Nothing Good or Bad in the Universe	29
	Three Levels of Existence	30
	"Sin" Means Ignorance	36

Chapter 3	**You Are Responsible**	**37**
	Awakening Humanity's Choices and Responsibility	37
	Free to Act or to React	38
	Fravashi: The Symbol—The Authentic Self	40
	The Symbol of Fravashi	43
	Gender Equality	45
Chapter 4	**The Purpose of Human Life**	**49**
	Wisdom Is Not Knowledge	49
	Consciousness and Mind: "Seeing" Is Not "Thinking"	51
	Happiness Is Not a State of Comfort	54
	Asha (Harmony and Balance): Both Internally and Externally	57
Chapter 5	**The Inner Alchemy**	**60**
	Mazdaism—The Followers of Wisdom	60
	A Few Principles of Mazdaism	61
Conclusion		**65**

About The Authors

This book is dedicated to all the wisdom keepers and seekers throughout the centuries who have contributed to awakening humanity. It is an attempt to bring together their wisdom, like a bee collecting the nectar of flowers for honey. As honey does not belong to one flower or one bee only, this book belongs to all the awakened people in history. It is the voice of all.

The author is Zarathustra Spitama (meaning "pure"), who lived five thousand years ago in Persia (Iran). For forty-seven years, he taught about wisdom and challenged the ignorance around him. He was murdered by the same people whom he tried to wake up.

The author is Yeshua (Jesus in Greek), who preached to people about love. He dedicated his life to curing people's inner eyes to see the truth and their inner ears to hear his wisdom. But there were no eyes to see, and no ears to hear him. At the end, he was crucified at the age of thirty-three by the ignorant people whom he tried to heal. His only crime was his love for humanity.

The author is Buddha (Siddhartha—his real name), who walked for forty years from village to village, telling people that there was a seed of a higher being within each of them that needed to be cultivated so that it would sprout and reach to the level of "Buddhahood"—The Awakened One.

The authors are Lao Tzu, Pythagoras, Socrates, Sufi mystics, like Hafiz, Rumi, and many others. Like a mail carrier who delivers the mail to your door, this book is just a package from all these enlightened people, prophets, awakened masters, and mystics who have contributed to the growth of humanity. They were all different fingers pointing to the same sun—higher wisdom.

Wisdom does not have any author, and no one can possess it. It is like no one can possess the sky; it belongs to all. Similarly, wisdom belongs to all and does not have an author, except wisdom itself. Zarathustra calls it Mazda—the Supreme Wisdom. Mazda is the only author of it. Upon seeing the beautiful sky, a musician composes, a painter paints it, and a poet writes poetry; every enlightened master looks at wisdom and describes it according to their own perception, language, culture, and gender. As the sky is the same, wisdom is not viewed differently by each of these awakened human beings. However, the explanation of it can be different. The sun is the same, but the fingers pointing to it are different. We fight about the fingers and whose finger is better than the other, and we miss looking at the sun to which all these fingers are pointing—the source of all light.

About The Authors

"The best life is for the one who turns towards light and sheds light to others."

(Zarathustra)

"He who in the First Beginning thus thought: Let the glorious heavens be clothed in light; He by His supreme understanding created the principles of Truth and Light."

(*Gathas*: Yasna 31.7)

"God made two great lights—the greater light to govern the day and the lesser light to govern the night. He also made the stars. God set them in the vault of the sky to give light on the earth, to govern the day and the night, and to separate light from darkness." (Gen. 1:15–18)

"This then is the message which we have heard of him, and declare unto you, that God is light, and in him is no darkness at all." (1 John 1:5)

"God is the Light of the heavens and earth. His Light is like this: there is a niche, and in it a lamp, the lamp inside a glass, a glass like a glittering star, fuelled from a blessed olive tree from neither east nor west, whose oil almost gives light even when no fire touches it - light upon light."

(Quran 24:35)

Acknowledgements

I would like to dedicate this book to my family in Canada and in Iran for their influence in my life. I am thankful for my Persian culture, which has taught me the wisdom of the East. I am indebted to the West and to Western culture and its people, who have hosted me kindly and lovingly over the past forty years of my life. I feel fortunate to have gained the wisdom of both the East and the West, like an eagle who has two wings, allowing me to fly as high as I have courage to. Together, these two cultures are like the right side and the left side of my brain. They help me to see and to understand life from a different point of view. They are not contradicting each other. Rather, they are complementary to one another. How fortunate can one be? I am so grateful to be exposed to both. This book is also dedicated to the beautiful, conscious new generation that is evolving now. It is a generation that knows nothing of herd mentality. They are seekers of truth.

I would like to offer this book also to all my clients whom I saw as a psychotherapist over the past thirty years. I am honoured to have had the privilege of encountering people who opened their hearts, their pains, their sufferings, and their joy to me. Once, I had a client who came for a final session, after having seen me for several years. Before she left my office, she smiled and said, "You know so much more about me than any other person. You know "my good, my bad, and my ugly."

It is true. I am a secret keeper. I keep many people's stories and vulnerabilities; parts which either no one dared to look at or did not feel safe to show to anyone else. Most people say to me, "It must be hard to be a therapist, sitting all day listening to people complaining." I say, "No, it is very hard for me when I leave the office and I am not a therapist anymore." Most people who want to be in therapy are their real selves in the session.

I always ask my clients to remove their shoes before walking on my Persian carpet in my office. In this way, I am symbolically asking them to remove their false self before entering this sacred room. "Come into this room barefoot, as authentic as you can be." My clients have been real, and I am thankful to all of them who opened themselves up and shared their inner lives with me. There is a saying which goes: "When a child is born, the parents are born." I am grateful to both my children and my clients for teaching me how to be a parent and a therapist. They were all my teachers. I learned from each of them.

This book is also dedicated to Fredrich Nietzsche (1844–1900), who introduced Zarathustra to the Western culture,[1] to French linguistic scholar Anqetil-Duperron (1731–1805), who translated the *Gathas* (Zarathustra Sublime Songs) so that we now have a clear understanding of the wisdom of Zarathustra for the first time after thousands of years, to German

---

[1] Unfortunately, his message was misinterpreted, misrepresented, and corrupted by his sister after his death and was misused in the hands of wicked people and spirits.

Acknowledgements

scholar Martin Haug (1827–1876), Osho, and Dr. Khosro Khazai (Pardis)[2], who separated the wisdom of Zarathustra from Zoroastrian religion, to British scholar Mary Boyce (1920–2006), who contributed many years of her life to the immense research and study of Zarathustra's wisdom, and to D. J. Irani[3] and Mobed Firouz Azargoshasb[4], whose translations of the *Gathas* are used as the source in this book. As a Persian, I am grateful to all of them for bringing Zarathustra's teachings back to life again.

I would like to thank my friend Ray for helping edit the book at times and for being a sounding board to explore my ideas when I needed it. I am grateful to have him as my friend. I would also like to express my gratitude to my dear friend Thomas for his loving, innocent heart and his healing power.

As a psychotherapist and a healer, I have sought out many therapists, psychologists, meditations, and workshops to work on myself for over thirty years. A healer needs healing more than anyone else. I travelled to India, went to Bud Gaya, where Buddha was enlightened, sat in his cave and under the Bodhi tree where he was meditating, spent time in ashram in India, attended many aboriginal sweat lodges and vision quests, practiced tantra, spent time with Sufis and their gatherings, and so on. However, something was not opening in me. I still felt a blockage within.

---

2 *The Gathas: The Sublime Book of Zarathustra* by Dr. Khosro Khazai (Pardis).
3 *The Gathas: The Hymns of Zarathustra* by D. J. Irani
4 *Translation of Gathas: The Holy Songs of Zarathustra* by Mobed Firouz Azargoshasb

I went to many of Thomas's healing sessions for over three years. However, nothing significant was happening in my core being. I needed something deeper, a DNA change, an awakening. On April 2, 2022, I was in one of Thomas's healing gatherings. He asked people to come for his healing ritual that he was performing that day. I went to him and felt something open in me, finally. He broke a dam in me, and I was flooded thereafter. It felt like he gave me a new birth. Interestingly, the day before that was April first—April Fool's Day. I felt that I was a fool all my life and was born again. Moterassed was an old me and Spitama[5] grew out of it. I was a caterpillar, and a butterfly began to emerge. I feel like a snake shading the old skin while the newer one is beginning to unfold.

> I died as mineral and became a plant,
> I died as plant and rose to animal,
> I died as animal and I was human,
> Why should I fear? When was I less by dying?
>
> Rumi

THANK YOU ALL

---

5 Spitama is chosen here because of the author's immense love and respect for the wisdom of Zarathustra Spitama.

Glossary

Ahriman	Wicked thought/Spirit/Energy/Anger *Angra Mainyu* in the *Gathas*, Satan in English
Ahura Mazda	The Sublime Wisdom, The Essence The Supreme Consciousness, God in English Both masculine and feminine *Ahura*: masculine, consciousness, light *Mazda*: feminine, wisdom, life
Angra Mainyu	The spirit of ignrance, unconsciousness Wickedness, anger in English, *Ahriman*, Satan in English
Asha/Artha	Harmony, balance, *Artha*, art in English, harmony
Daena	Conscience, inner wisdom and morality, inner eyes Deen/Din: Religion in Persian
Fravashi	Authentic self, true self/spirit, our essence "I" Angel, guardian angel in English, "Holy Souls"

Gathas	Songs, the Sublime Songs of Zarathustra Composed by himself about 5,000 years ago The only surviving language of Indo-European
Magi	The followers of Zarathustra's wisdom teaching Seeker of wisdom, *Moghan* in Persian, *Magi* in Greek Zoroastrian priests (*Mobed*)
Mainyu	Mind in English, spirit, energy, way of thinking
Serosha	Conscience voice, inner voice
Spenta	Sacred, holy, progressive
Spenta Mainyu	Sacred wisdom, good mind, progressive mentality Holy Spirit in English
Spitama	Zarathustra also known as, meaning "pure"
Zarathustra	Zarathustra was an enlightened person who lived about 5,000 years ago in Persia (Iran). The founder Zoroastrian religion and Mazdaism (seeker of Wisdom).

Introduction

An Unconscious Existence

> "Unto you, O Creator, the Soul of Mother Earth complained thus: Wherefore did you create me? Who gave life to me? Anger, rapine, outrage, blunder, aggression and violence are everywhere. There is no protector for me, except Thee. Therefore, reveal to me a savior who could show me a way out of this difficulty."
>
> (*Gathas*: Yasna 29.1)

We live in a time when the world is in chaos. Our air, water, soil, and animals are rapidly being contaminated and destroyed. The population on our planet is exploding, and greed is diminishing the natural resources. There is more hunger and poverty in many different nations. Hate is growing among different ethnic and racial groups. We are becoming fearful of others who are different than us. There is more concern globally of aggression and hatred in the name of God and religion. Our movies and entertainment are full of violence and crime. The only difference between us and the Romans who were watching gladiators fighting and killing each other as entertainment is location. We are not watching it anymore at the Coliseum; we watch it from the comfort of our homes and movie theatres while eating popcorn.

In this chaotic and fast-paced life we are experiencing these days, it becomes an expectation that our importance in most societies is to "run fast" and to get ahead of someone else in a global rat race. Like a hamster on a wheel, everyone runs faster daily, imagining they are getting somewhere. However, we need to realize that we are running on a hamster wheel. The faster one runs, the faster the wheel turns.

There was once a king walking in his garden who saw a beggar sitting next to the wall near the garden. The king was in a good mood that day and went to the beggar. He told him to ask for whatever he desired, and the king would give it to him. The beggar looked at the king and said, "You are more of a beggar than me. I am fine after getting my meal for the day. But you are such a beggar that no matter what you conquer, or what you have, it is never enough for you. You keep begging for more."

What we need in such chaos in the world and on our planet is not more division, hatred, or greed. Humanity requires unity and wisdom. We need to search for universal principles and values that can embrace us all together and guide us toward becoming loving, conscious human beings. It is important to remember to be more compassionate toward our planet and other living things on it. We are still like prisoners trapped in the prison of our ignorance, vanity, deceptions, and greed. To escape our prison, we must help each other, have a map, a plan, and leadership to assist us toward our liberation. We also need the wisdom of other enlightened masters who have already escaped from this unconscious jail.

It is important for each of us to realize that we are not human yet. It is not a sign of our humanity that we stand and walk on our legs, use tools, speak a language, have a higher intelligence, or have values and morality. We can only call ourselves human beings when we live consciously and our hearts are filled with love and compassion. We are like caterpillars in a cocoon of time, transforming into human beings. To accomplish this transition, we need a guide, certain principles, willpower, aim, and sincerity.

If a person is seeing a therapist, it means they are not functioning well. Similarly, if one sees a doctor, it means the person is ill. We don't see our therapist because we feel great and simply want to grow as a human being. We don't see a doctor because we feel healthy and only want the doctor to keep us in good health. The dictionary defines health as "the absence of illness." There is no definition of what "health" is. In ancient China, people used to see their healers to keep them healthy. It's like going to the gym regularly not because we are sick but rather with the intention of keeping ourselves healthy. The approach in healing needs to be directed toward growth and being aware of our "being" rather than our "doing." The purpose of our growth as a human is to integrate self-awareness and self-observation within our everyday lives. Observation means "being aware with no thoughts, with no inner talking, with no chattering inside; just remaining with what is as it is."

The aim of our healing and growth needs to go beyond focussing on dysfunction around life events and problems, toward self-actualization and personal growth. We have moved away from the teaching of ancient wisdom keepers turning instead to psychotherapy and pharmaceutical medications. The focus of Western psychotherapy is to keep people functional. However, to be functional in life is not enough. Just functioning daily is not of any significance. It means living a repetitive and a routine life and having the capacity to cope with our struggles. It does not give meaning, and insight into the reality of our being, and it does not take anyone near their full potential. A robot or a car can function better than a human. But they are not alive; they are not evolving into higher beings.

The purpose of the Eastern approach and wisdom of the awakened masters and prophets is not to make people functional. The focus is to transform humanity into their higher and conscious selves. Healing is about changing our level of being. Being is who we really are and to change it, we must not just be satisfied with who we are. A person needs to continuously work toward becoming. A caterpillar can never transform into a butterfly if it is happy to be a caterpillar.

Our World Needs Wisdom

>Yesterday a wise master carrying a lit lantern in daylight was looking around town saying, "I am weary of all 'unconscious people.' I seek a 'true' human being."
>They said, "There is none, we too have searched before."
>'The one who is not to be found easily is my desire,' the master replied.
>
>(Rumi)

Introduction

Enlightened masters have come to disturb us from our deep and cozy sleep. We think of ourselves as awake, conscious beings. This is often a lie. When we examine ourselves deeply, we discover that we are not as conscious as we believe we are. We unconsciously sleep several hours a day, and when we are awake during the day we may function unconsciously and mechanically. We think that we are awake, but we are not. We function throughout our day like robots. How often do you drive and are conscious of your driving? We often drive without being aware of driving. The body drives robotically, but our mind is somewhere else, like an Alzheimer's patient, physically there, but mentally absent.

How often do you eat, walk, talk, or shower consciously, fully aware of all your senses? If we watch ourselves, we realize that often we are on autopilot. Our body performs a task, but our mind is absent. We are often not fully present in our lives. Thoughts come and go. Emotions and feelings come and go. We move and talk and eat and act without being aware. Are we conscious human beings?

When we observe ourselves consciously within, there is not a singular person inside but a mob that we mistakenly call "I." We are continuously being hijacked by different emotions or thoughts throughout the day without any awareness. Someone asked Buddha, "How can I practice consciousness?" He said, "Just observe your breath without any thoughts or emotion for five minutes." The person said, "That is it? This is very easy." Buddha said, "Yes, it is easy to say, but very hard to do."

So often we speak of Truth, with a capital *T*, as if it was static. Truth means something is pure and innocent, without any fabrication. The sun rises in the east and sets in the west. It does not need proof. It just needs eyes to see it and to be witnessed. There are two kinds of truths: an objective truth and a subjective truth. There is a difference between a scientist and a mystic. A scientist looks at truth as either-or, black or white, right or wrong. This is an external objective truth. A chair is a chair, and it is not a car. A mystic, on the other hand, searches for truth's complexity in a mystical and subjective way, like a child full of wonder and curiosity. One needs to be present and conscious to see things as they are without contaminating them with judgement, ideas, or thoughts. To see the truth, we need to look at it as if through the eyes of a child. Children look at everything with innocent eyes, a beginner's eyes.

In Zen, there is a saying that "one cannot speak of truth. The moment it is spoken, it becomes a lie." To look at things consciously means to see everything as in a mirror: it is what it is. Truth is not like a gold which we can find and claim to possess. Truth evolves eternally. It is always beyond our grasp. There is always more. It is like a horizon—as you try to get closer to it, it goes further. Like the horizon that we cannot possess, we can never reach a point to hold on to the truth. We just need to look at it openly and consciously. The moment we hold on to the truth, it becomes like a plastic flower. It is not alive anymore. It looks good, but it is a dead truth; it is a mummified truth.

Wisdom is open and flows like a river. We think when someone is wise, they know everything. That is not the case. A wise person can only see things as they are, without judgement, and respond to them consciously rather than robotically. The river is fresh as opposed to a pool because it is always moving.

Introduction

It is not stagnated like a pond. Wisdom is the state of being—open and not stuck in truth like a rock. Wisdom means to stand at the river and look at its flow. It is the state of not looking at the frozen river but looking at the truth and life accordingly, with open and curious eyes.

There is a difference between wisdom and knowledge. Wisdom is inner truth and knowing based on one's existential experience. It does not come from outside of us through reading scriptures, books, or going to university and gathering information. Wisdom grows in the depth of our consciousness and life experiences. Wisdom is pure and innocent. Knowledge is the mind's function. It is gathering information externally by accumulating and memorizing it in the mind. Through knowledge, we become knowledgeable, not wise. Wisdom is like a well, where the water comes from within from an inner source. Knowledge is like a pool that one needs to keep maintaining and adding to it from outside.

A person might have a PhD, but it does not mean they are wise. Yeshua (Jesus in Greek)[6] did not have a degree from any university nor was he as "knowledgeable" as the priests (Pharisees) that he was challenging. But he had wisdom. Knowledge creates thoughts in the mind, but wisdom expands our consciousness. Knowledge means to think, but wisdom means to see and to know. That is why most of the wisdom keepers have come to help us to "see." They have come to cure not our

---

6   The name Yeshua rather than Jesus has been chosen for this book. It needs to be pointed out that Jesus's real name was "Yeshua" in Hebrew and Joshua in English. The name Jesus was given to him by the Greeks years after his crucifixion. However, Jesus's real name was "Yeshua." https://en.wikipedia.org/wiki/Jesus_(name)

external eyes, but rather our internal eyes, to cure our internal blindness—our ignorance. However, it is important in life to have both knowledge and wisdom, like a bird with two wings. We gain knowledge to drive a car, to do a heart surgery, or to build a house. However, knowledge is not enough in one's life. We also need to gain wisdom to not make the same mistake again, to raise our children, to be with each other in a healthier way, and to find who we really are; not as who we are, rather, whom we have the potential to become.

The more open and receptive we are, the more truth and wisdom we can receive. We cannot create truth; our inner work is to keep ourselves open like a container and fill ourselves with more of it. It is impossible to plant an oak tree in a small pot, nor can we pour an ocean into a mug. To receive the truth, we need to have openness, willingness, and receptiveness.

The Truth Will Set You Free, but it Will Hurt

A problem with our information-rich technological societies is that there is so much information and sadly little wisdom. Information is at our fingertips, and it is tempting to think that we know all there is to know. In our information bubbles there is no room for other perspectives. Our hard drives are too full; often full of junk that we don't even know that we have picked up along the way. We are like camels burdened by too many weights and the burden of other's beliefs loaded on us since we were a child. There is a Buddhist tea story in which a wise monk serves tea to an aspiring student. The monk continues to pour the tea even when the cup overflows. Wondering why, the monk explains to the student that he came filled with so much knowledge that there was no room for curiosity, no room for new insights, no room for deeper wisdom.

Perhaps, we need to unload ourselves from all past imposed education, truth, and beliefs and re-examine all our "knowing" from the start again. It comes to a point in our lives that we need to die as a Phoenix and be reborn again. However, this time our birth comes from our own *"truth"* from our own *"search"* from our own *"discovery."* Hopefully, we all come to a point in our lives when we say, *"Enough of being a camel. I want to be Buddah, Yeshua (Jesus), Zarathustra, an awakened one. I want to choose my destiny and who truly I am. I don't want to be a sheep. I want to be a shepherd in my life."*

Tell Me the Truth, but Don't Tell Me the Truth

As a therapist I once had a family therapy session with parents and their teenage son. The parents discovered that their teenager had been smoking marijuana for a few months, and they were upset that he had lied about it. Their goal in therapy was for me to work with their son so that he would be truthful. During an individual session the teenager admitted that he had been smoking pot for five years. I encouraged him to be honest with his parents. Hesitantly, he agreed, and in the next session he told the truth, as his parents had requested.

The parents were furious and began shouting during the session. After a few minutes I turned to the son and said, *"Don't tell the truth to your parents anymore! Don't tell them the truth until they are ready to handle your truth telling."* Like those parents, are we ready for new truths or to explore deeper wisdom? The writer of the Gospel of John said, *"The truth will set you free."* The truth will set you free but first it will hurt and make you miserable. It hurts to let go of what you believed to be true before. Comfort is easier to seek than truth. Truth is disturbing. Opening ourselves up to the truth hurts because we must let go of what we have believed in. That is why society kills the truth keepers like Zarathustra or Yeshua. We murder them hoping to kill the "truth." We can murder them, but one cannot kill the truth. It will emerge again like the spring after a long winter period. Winter cannot kill spring. It only holds spring until the time comes to appear fresh again. Truth is like spring. It is always fresh, alive and pregnant with so many possibilities and potential.

Intention

One of the main purposes of this book is to stay away from herd-mentality and to follow what has been known blindly. Questioning, doubting, examining, and re-evaluating our beliefs is the beginning of one's growth. This book is intended to create reflections and questions for the readers rather than providing an answer or an intellectual and academic discussion about religion and spirituality.

Humanity is slowly drowning in a quicksand of consumerism and meaninglessness despite all its scientific and technological achievements. We need to create a humanity that rises above the current circumstances. The teachings and guidance of enlightened masters such as Buddha, Yeshua (Jesus), Zarathustra, and Lao Tzu are more important now than ever to lead us toward a higher consciousness. Let's allow the truth to be like a mother embracing us all, regardless of our differences, in her arms to nourish our hungry souls with the milk of wisdom. Let's pause for a bit in our busy days and search for truth, as all the enlightened masters have guided us to for centuries.

We cannot reach our ultimate potential if we resist change and ignore our inner seeds of wisdom. "And no one pours new wine into old wineskins. Otherwise, the wine will burst the skins, and both the wine and the wineskins will be ruined."[7] No, they pour new wine into new wineskins. Yeshua, Buddha, and Zarathustra's fresh wisdom teachings did not fit into the minds of the religious leaders of their times (old wineskins). One needs to pour their living teachings into the "new wineskins," of those whose minds are as thirsty and hungry as a child's. All our lights need to come together and become the sun in this darkness we are entering. It is time to wake up. Although there is a voice of many awakened ones expressed here, Zarathustra's teachings have been explored more as the foundation of many other wisdom keepers. The book is contributed to him: *Zarathustra Spitama*.

Although he lived about 5,000 years ago in Central Asia (Persia), he was ahead of his time. His message and teachings were meant for this generation. He had an "awakened spirit," and he planted the seeds of consciousness years ago for our time to come. Like Yeshua (Jesus) who brought Lazarus back to life from the cave, perhaps this book can bring the wisdom of Zarathustra that has been forgotten and kept in the cave of history for centuries back to life once more.

---

7   Mark 2:22. NIV

Zarathustra tells us to seek the truth everywhere. Don't limit yourself in your search for the truth. Go see what Buddha says; what Moses and Yeshua say. Be like a desert, waiting for a drop of truth to fall and quench your thirsty soul. Be open to including different pieces of the puzzle of many truths, whether you agree or disagree, whether it hurts you or comforts you. Truth is much more like a verb, rather than a noun. It is more relative than static.

> "With an open mind, seek and listen to all the highest ideals. Consider the most enlightened thoughts. Then choose your path, person by person, each for oneself."
>
> (*Gathas:* Yasna 30.2)

Let's get together, like being near a fireplace, where we can all pause, warm up, be open, listen, and reflect upon it. The concept that has been presented here is only a finger pointing to your own inner wisdom, where all the answers are stored. Wisdom is Zarathustra's aim in his teachings, awakening us to who we really are. He is a gardener encouraging us to plant the seed of our existence to bloom to a higher conscious being. He does not see us as a caterpillar. He sees in each of us the potential of being a butterfly. Zarathustra is not here to impose himself on us; rather, he is a loving father, a teacher, and a guide who brings us all under the same roof, despite our differences. He is not a "guru," but rather an alarm clock to wake us up to the dawn of our true existence. He is just a rooster crowing to wake us up from our deep sleep. He never asks anyone to follow him. He does not need followers—he asks you to follow your own intelligence, your own wisdom, your own consciousness.

CHAPTER 1
Zarathustra

Zaroaster (Zarathustra) painted by Pajaros Volando

The Wise Zarathustra

You great star, what would your happiness be had you not those for whom you shine? For ten years you have climbed to my cave: you would have tired of your light and of the journey had it not been for me and my eagle and my serpent. But we waited for you every morning, took your overflow from you, and blessed you for it. Behold, I am weary of my wisdom, like a bee that has gathered too much honey; I need hands outstretched to receive it. I would give away and distribute, until the wise among men find joy once again in their folly, and the poor in their riches.

(*Thus Spake Zarathustra*–Fredrich Nietzsche)

Zarathustra is mostly known in the West by Fredrich Nietzche's book, *Thus Spake Zarathustra*. Throughout history, Zarathustra's teachings have shaped and impacted different cultures and belief systems through a wide variety of ways worldwide. In addition to Nietzsche, Mozart's opera *The Magic Flute*, with its core themes of searching for truth and the pursuit of wisdom and goodness above all, was also influenced by Zarathustra's teachings. Richard Strauss, a German composer, composed *Also Sprach Zarathustra* in 1896. In 1968, the symphony became well known after it was used in the movie, *2001: A Space Odyssey*. Freddie Mercury, the talented and innovative singer of rock music (Queen), proudly expressed his Persian Zoroastrian roots throughout his life. The cosmic battle between the Light and Dark sides of the Force in *Star Wars* has been immensely inspired by Zoroastrian religion."[8] The name Mazda car company comes from *Ahura Mazda* (Lord of Wisdom), the Zoroastrian God of harmony, consciousness, and intelligence. Zoroastrianism was known in Japanese as a peaceful religion. The name was chosen as a symbol of the beginning of the East and the West civilizations.[9]

8   The obscure religion that shaped the West, BBC Culture 2017   https://www.bbc.com/culture/article/20170406-this-obscure-religion-shaped-the-west
9   A Story Behind the Name of "Mazda" https://www.mazda.com/en/innovation/mazda-stories/mazda/behind

Chapter 1   Zarathustra

Buddha's name was Siddhartha, and he was named Buddha (the awakened one) later, after his enlightenment. Similarly, Zarathustra was the title given to him after his enlightenment. *Zaratha* means gold (*zar* in Persian) and *ushtra* means light (star in Persian ستاره). He was known also as *Spitama (Pure)*. Zarathustra means "the one who possesses the Golden Light." The word "enlightenment" was later used as a spiritual term after his name.

The magi were followers of Zarathustra's wisdom teaching. They were seekers of wisdom, *moghan* in Persian, *magi* in Greek. Zoroastrian priests were known as *"mobed,"* from the same root. "Often, they were skilled in astrology, cosmology, psychology, meditation, herbology, alchemy, and had remarkable healing abilities. The word magic comes from magi for their extraordinary power of healing and wisdom. The magi exercised positions of power in Persian politics because of their wisdom."[10] The magi in the Gospel of Matthew were Zoroastrian priests who were following "the shining/golden star" in search of their messiah (Saoshyant) as Zarathustra promised people to come after him.

The Persian mystic poet Hafiz (fourteenth century) wrote of the wisdom of the magi gathered in Zarathustra's inner circle in his time as *'The Divine Light."*

> *In the tavern of the Magi, I see the bright light of Divine*
> *O what a light, such a delight, how can it so brightly shine?*
> *Stop showing off to me, O pilgrim of the House of God*

---

10   *Original Magic: The Rituals and Initiation of the Persian Magi* by Dr. Stephen E. Flowers, 2017

In that place you see the house, while I see God's grand design.
Secrets of the divine, for myself I wish to define
This is a mindless design, myself I further misalign.

(Hafiz, Ghazal 357)

Zarathustra was himself a magi priest, originally in an ancient Mithraic temple. However, he shifted his attitude toward the priestly profession after his enlightenment and had little value for their use of excessive robotic rituals. He challenged the hypocrisy of the priests and was killed forty-seven years after his revelation, when Mazdaism was already well established by the magi—his followers.[11]

It is difficult to establish an exact date for Zarathustra's life since very little is known about it. It appears that the best method to arrive at a date for his life comes from a study of the language spoken in the hymns he composed himself in the *Gathas* (songs). However, most scholars believe that he lived approximately 5000 to 7000 years ago. The *Gathas* is a compilation of hymns. It is one of the oldest languages that has survived to our time. Listening to the songs of the *Gathas*, one can get a glimpse of how Indo-Europeans used to speak. Some of the words used are similar to English. For instance, Angra means anger. Mainyu means mind, and Asha (Artha—harmony and balance) means art.

Zarathustra's teachings were unique and progressive for his time, when violence, slavery, and oppression were dominating human lives. He was extremely concerned with what he

---

[11] *The Zoroastrian Tradition: An Introduction to the Ancient Wisdom of Zarathustra* by Farhang Mehr

witnessed: a disgrace of the human spirit, cruelty to animals, and a devastation of the environment. He challenged people and corruption around him, not by force, authority, or violence, but rather, he sought to shift them through reason, wisdom, and awareness. Zarathustra dreamt of a society and earth where people were empowered to think for themselves and to choose their destiny instead of being blind followers. He opposed a herd mentality and a robotic thinking, and he encouraged people to seek wisdom and knowledge from the enlightened individuals. He saw the inherent goodness in each person and encouraged them to seek goodness in their thoughts, words, and actions.

The teachings of Mazdaism and Zarathustra are universal and very clear: good thought, good word, and good deed. It is a way and a path of wisdom. The focus is to embrace consciousness and goodness in our existence. Ahura Mazda is the source and essence of the wisdom within us. His teachings are based on freedom of choice, intelligence, and consciousness. Zarathustra's personification of *Ahura Mazda* was not a tribal, punishing God, but rather a spirit within humanity guiding all to a joyous and harmonious life on earth; governed by kindness, truth, and wisdom in both balance of masculine and feminine within and outside of us. His religion was known for centuries as "Good Religion."[12]

The first principle of Zarathustra to understand is that we humans are not conscious; don't have a sense of unity within; don't know who we are; and are incomplete. To begin with, one needs to realize how much we live in unawareness. Unless

---

12   *The Good Religion* by Stephen E. Flowers, 2014.

everyone becomes conscious, there will always remain a need for some kind of ethical guidance to keep humanity intact.

Zarathustra did not believe in a revolution, rather, he invited us to experience an evolution and an inner change. Revolution is external, changing one system of governing to a different one. Evolution is very internal. It is based on one's inner growth from ignorance to consciousness. It is one's degree of consciousness and awareness. All revolutions have failed so far, from the time of Spartacus to Marxism and Socialism. They failed because the people who succeeded the previous ruling system were as unconscious as those before them.

Zarathustra came to bring higher consciousness so that people can live based on their own inner conscience (Daenâ), not on the higher ethical codes imposed upon them. His morality is like a mathematical formula. When one learns it, the person can apply it in many areas and moments in life: *good thoughts, good words, and good deeds.* Except for a small number of awakened individuals, humanity has pretended to be like human beings. Deep down in our psyche, we are nothing but more sophisticated animals, pretending to be human beings. If one scratches a bit under the surface, the animal part of us comes out immediately. For instance, the moment the lights of New York City went out on July 13, 1977, more than 1600 stores (groceries, drugstores, or clothing shops) were robbed by so-called "civilized people" during the blackout. In fact, this example was not a technical issue but a social failure.[13]

Religion teaches the idea of right and wrong, should and shouldn't, pure and impure. Zarathustra takes us beyond all purity and impurity, right and wrong. Mazda and wisdom are beyond all of that. Zarathustra continuously targeted the hypocrisy of the religious leaders of their times. And he was murdered by hypocritical and virtuous priests. A virtue, according to Zarathustra, should be based on one's intelligence, logic, and wisdom. An important element of his vision is free will. This means that he emphasized the moral responsibility of the individual. Every decision people make is an opportunity to serve either "Good" (Mazda, light, and consciousness) or "Bad" (Ahriman, darkness, and unconsciousness).

Light and fire became symbols of his teachings. They are symbols of the initial fire of creation, the internal fire, consciousness, wisdom, goodness, and the energy of action. Zarathustra's religion is based on the *"inner fire"* of one's level of awareness and consciousness that needs to be burning continuously to bring light within and without. As he said, *"The best life is for the one who turns towards light and sheds light to others."* He encourages people to be aware of the inner fire and light of their consciousness and to respond to every

---

13 The Washington Post. Democracy Dies in Darkness: How the 1977 blackout unleashed New York City's tough-on-crime politics. The lights went out for a day. The consequences lasted decades. By Analysis by Kim Phillips-Fein. July 2017. https://www.washingtonpost.com/news/made-by-history/wp/2017/07/13/the-1977-blackout-led-to-new-york-citys-tough-on-crime-politics/

circumstance in their lives spontaneously, not according to any scripture, but according to their inner wisdom.

Zarathustra is like an alchemist who transforms a "base metal" into a higher substance (gold). His teaching is transcending humanity to conscious individuals. The lower unconscious humanity needs to die within in order to give birth to the higher being. He calls this inner alchemy developing a *"new character"* within. He saw the true potential of humanity as a seed that needs to go beyond itself. Human beings can only call themselves human when they are not entangled with the seed of who they already are and are able to transcend themselves into the flower of their conscious beings. According to his teachings, the transcending of oneself from a lower consciousness to the higher one is the purpose of humanity on Earth. He did not preach against the pleasure of life or renouncing the world, rather he was an awakened human being who spent his life to awaken us.

Zarathustra was only extraordinary in his ordinary being, and his complexity was in the simplicity of his teachings. He created the path of Mazdaism—the followers of "truth." He experienced Ultimate Wisdom through a mystical experience and contemplation in his inner being.

> *"O, Lord of Life and Wisdom, when I realized Thee in my mind as the First and the Last of Creation, then I found with my inner sight (conscience). As I have seen Ahura Mazda with my inner sight, I shall strive to draw His attention towards myself with songs of praise."*
>
> (*Gathas:* Yasna 31.8)

His teachings also established the religion of Zoroastrianism. It became the dominant religion of the Persian Empires: The Achaemenid (c. 550–330 BCE), Parthians (c. 247 BCE–224 CE), and Sasanian (224–651 CE). It remained the state religion of the Persian Empire until about the seventh century CE, when Muslims conquered Persia. Due to several invasions by Greeks, Arabs, and Mongols in Persia, many of the wisdom teachings and esoteric schools were destroyed. Due to changes in the Persian language throughout its history, Zarathustra's hymns (the *Gathas*) were not understood until the eighteenth-century CE when Anquetil-Duperron, a French linguistic scholar, translated them into French.

Ahura Mazda: The Union of Consciousness and Wisdom

As we have seen, Ahura Mazda (The Supreme Wisdom, The Essence, Spirit of all Spirits, The Absolute) means wisdom, consciousness, or perhaps life itself. The fact that Zarathustra used the sun as a metaphor for Ahura Mazda has created some confusion. Some have wrongfully assumed that Zarathustra and his followers were sun worshipers. This is not accurate. The sun is used merely as a metaphor to explain Mazda's (wisdom) relationship to the rest of the universe.

> "What shall Thou, O God, bestow upon us through Thy spiritual lights?"
>
> *(Gathas:* Yasna 31.3)

> *"We yearn for Thy mighty light which is shining through truth, O Lord of Life. The shining blaze which is eternal and powerful. The light which guides the followers of truth clearly and helps them."*
>
> *(Gathas:* Yasna 34.4)

As the sun is the centre of our solar system and everything moves around it, The Supreme Wisdom is the centre of the authentic existence of all human beings. In similar fashion to gravity, the radiance of Ahura Mazda holds us all together. Nothing in the universe is separate. There is no separate existence apart from Ahura Mazda (The Sublime Wisdom), as there is no separation between one's head, heart, lungs, or feet. Although they all appear to be apart, they are all part of the body. They are all interconnected as a whole.

> "The Essences are each a separate Glass
> Through which the Sun of Being's Light is passed.
> Each tinted fragment Sparkles in the Sun
> A thousand colors but the Light is One.
>
> (Persian poet, Jami)

Ahura Mazda can exist and shine without us, but we cannot exist without it. There are two qualities of the sun: warmth and light. Every planet receives the light and warmth of the sun varying based on their position in the solar system. The further from the sun a planet is, the less light and less warmth it receives. No planet or moon has its own warmth and light. So, there is no such thing as moonlight. The moon only reflects the light of the sun. The farther from wisdom and consciousness within us, the more ignorant and unconscious our lives would be.

As the sun's rays give light and warmth to the planets, Mazda also gives the rays of love and wisdom to existence unconditionally. If it is a sunny day and we are sitting in a dark basement, it does not mean that the sun is withholding its light and warmth from us. We just need to get out to where the sun shines. Depending on our level of maturity and our closeness to Ahura Mazda, we will receive more, or less, love and wisdom. As the sun radiates light and warmth to the darkness and coldness of Earth and brings life to it, Ahura Mazda also radiates life to every living being and to the darkness of our ignorance and unconsciousness. As the light of Earth cannot exist without the sun, there is no life apart from the illumination of The Supreme Being.

The distance between us and The Supreme Wisdom is not external; it is in the depth of our core beings like H2O and water. It is like water is seeking to find H2O outside itself. The whole existence and essence of water is H2O—hydrogen and oxygen. Ahura Mazda is our essence, like H2O. Therefore, the connection of us to it is not physical, but mental. It is like someone who has been in a coma for many years. The person does not need to seek consciousness outside the self. The person needs to be awakened; to connect within the self, to remember himself or herself. As many spiritual schools point out: "It is a path of self-remembering."

The ancient magi who were the true followers of Mazdaism saw Ahura Mazda as Light—the oldest conception of God. It is the Light around and within us. For Zarathustra, the contrast of light and darkness is only a metaphor for the state of consciousness and ignorance (unconsciousness). The worship of magi for fire is only symbolic, and it is a metaphor of the eternal flame burning in the temple of our bodies. The fire, however, has never been worshipped by Zarathustra and his followers.

> *"That light which is the light of faith do Thou, O Mazda Ahura, who art always the same, brighten in our hearts."*
>
> *(Gathas:* Yasna 31.7)

The God Within

The songs in the *Gathas* are the inner dialogue of Zarathustra with his inner wisdom. He did not see The Sublime Wisdom outside himself, but within. *"As I have seen Ahura Mazda with my inner sight."* He was one with The Absolute Being.

> "O, Lord of Life and Wisdom, when I realized
> Thee in my mind as the First and the Last of Creation."
>
> *(Gathas:* Yasna 45.8)

We misunderstand Zarathustra's teachings completely if we reduce them to a dialogue with a being outside of himself. The wisdom he found was through his inner voice (*Serosha*) and inner ears. He was like a diver who searched in the depths of the ocean to find a pearl. He dove into the depths of his own consciousness to find that pearl of wisdom (Mazda) within. The real self is nothing more than Mazda. He encouraged everyone to go into the depth of their own being and to find wisdom (Mazda) in the vastness of their own consciousness.

The Twin Spirits: Unity, Not Duality

Zarathustra speaks of a twin force at work in the world and in human consciousness. The first one is the Good Mind (*Spenta Mainyu,* The Sacred Wisdom), which wants to pull us to a higher consciousness (Wisdom). This is the force of progression. The other force is called the Wicked Mind (*Angra Mainyu,* Destructive Force, evil in English). This internal force wants to pull us down to ignorance, destruction, and unconsciousness. This is the spirit of stagnation and deception. These two forces are not opposite to each other or in a cosmic struggle. They are related to one another as a pair.

> "In the beginning there were two primal spirits, twins spontaneously active. These are the Good and the Evil, in thought, and in word, and in deed. Between these two, let the wise choose right. Be good, not bad."
>
> (*Gathas:* Yasna 30.3)

The best analogy is that of an elastic band. The more one pulls the elastic in one direction, the more another force tries to pull in the opposite direction. We cannot know one force unless we experience the other force. We don't know darkness if we have not seen light. One thinks that a person born blind lives in darkness. This is not true. Someone who is born blind cannot know darkness since he or she has not yet experienced light. We don't know cold unless we know hot. These two forces are not opposite; they are in relation with each other. They complete each other. They are complementary. We humans grow and learn through our experiences of these two forces; forces which offer us choices. We don't know what is good unless we experience something bad.

Ahriman (Evil)

Evil means dullness and emptiness. It does not have a quality. It lacks any quality. Darkness does not have its own substance. It lacks light. Ignorance does not have its own substance. It lacks wisdom and consciousness. It is the state of darkness of the mind. Wisdom is viewed as the light of the mind (enlightenment). Hate does not have its own attribute; it lacks love. Evil, or Ahriman, according to Zarathustra, means a state of dullness, stagnation, and lies. Lies means lack of truth; whatever that is not real. It lacks congruence, authenticity. Evil is not a person or entity. It is a state being that lacks light, consciousness, progression, and goodness. It is a state of emptiness and absence of goodness. It does not contain any truth. It is absolute lies. There is no such thing as a bit of truth or a little lie. A little truth is still a lie—Ahriman (lie, drugh in Persian). Truth and wisdom are God (Ahura Mazda). Lies and ignorance are Ahriman (evil), according to Zarathustra.

Hell and Heaven

In Zarathustra's view, hell and heaven are not geographical spaces where one goes after death. The concept is very symbolic. It is a state of mind that one creates for self and others as the result of a person's condition of thoughts, words, and actions. Heaven and hell exist mainly within us. Heaven is the purity of good thoughts, words, and deeds. There is no external punishment of burning in hell forever or being rewarded in heaven. We all need to understand that our good or evil thoughts, words, and deeds are preparing and shaping our destiny.

One always harvests what one sows. We cannot expect to have an orange when we plant an apple tree. Nor can we have a rose flower when we sow weeds. The more wisdom one gains, the greater the person's ability to recognize right from wrong. Wisdom can be defined as the ability to distinguish between good and evil, between right and wrong, truth and lies. Every person must use reason, intuition, and logic so they do not walk blindly. Hell and heaven are the creation that we live based on the choices we make.

> *"In truth, the person who shows us the path of truth and happiness in the corporeal world and saves the soul in the spiritual one shall attain the highest good. The said path is that which leads us to the real and true world, where Ahura is."*
>
> (*Gathas:* Yasna 43.3)

CHAPTER 2
Free to Choose

The Choice Is Yours

> "May the people, O Lord of Life, give ear to a wise man whose teachings are soul heating and beneficial and act according to them in their lives. May they listen to the person who is capable of spreading the religion of truth and has eloquence of speech. Through Thy radiant fire, O Lord of Wisdom, do assign the densities of both parties [the wise and the ignorant].
>
> (*Gathas:* Yasna 31.19)

From the beginning of time, two primal spirits have been spontaneously active in our lives. In thought, word, or deed one leads toward good and wise, another toward bad and foolish. Between these two, let the wise choose to be good, not foolish! This idea has been passed along to humanity in many forms. One such story speaks of twin wolves living inside us. One leads us to good thoughts, good words, and good deeds, while the other to lies and pain. Which one will win? The one that you decide to feed.

Chapter 2   Free to Choose

Two Sides of a Coin

Zarathustra teaches us about two forces in human minds (Conscious Mind and Wicked Mind). They're in a complementary position with each other, like two sides of a coin. You cannot take one side of a coin and destroy it and forget about the other side. Both exist together simultaneously. A man and woman are one soul in two different bodies. They are two sides of the same coin. Night and day are not opposing each other; they're not fighting. Night completes day, and day completes the night. Winter and summer are not fighting with each other. They are moving in a circle and complete each other. This is not dualism. The cosmic battle between these forces and the separation of them from one another are foreign to the teachings of Zarathustra.

Nothing Good or Bad in the Universe

> "And when these Twin Spirits came together at first, They established Life and the Denial of Life; and so shall it be till the world will last."
>
> (*Gathas:* Yasna 30.4)

These twin forces exist only within the human mind. There is nothing good or bad in the universe. When a tiger kills a deer, it is not an act of evil. It is just an act of nature. When an earthquake destroys a town, it is not because God is punishing the villagers. It happens because of a shift in Earth's crust. People are not inherently bad or evil, based on Zarathustra's teachings.

There is no original sin in his teachings. What we choose makes us who we are and who we become. This is positive, good news; we are not locked into our past behaviour or mistakes. We always can change. A sinner can become a saint and a saint can be a sinner in a split second. A "sinner" may jump to the water to save someone's life knowing that they may die. And a saint can act harmfully at some point to the self or others and become a "sinner." Our existence on Earth is like a tightrope walker. Any minute we can take a totally different choice that is beyond our imagination. Each choice provides an opportunity to move in a more positive direction. Whosoever makes his or her mind better or worse, it will reflect on their thoughts, words, and deeds.

> "Whosoever makes his mind better or worse, his words and deeds show his way of thinking. He chooses for himself – at the end, in your wisdom, will he stand apart (depending on the choice made)."[14]
>
> (*Gathas:* Yasna 48.4)

Three Levels of Existence

In Zarathustra's view, there are three levels of existence living simultaneously together: 1. Mazda, 2. Spirit World (Mind, Maiynu), and 3. Matter. Although Mazda is a spirit, it is The Supreme Spirit (The Sublime Wisdom). It is the Spirit of all being and not being, of life and death. Mazda is The Essence

---

14 The Inner Fire, Nariman, Rohinton F.

of all beings. It is like an apple tree: one cannot see where the apple seed is when it has grown into an apple tree. The seed has already dissolved into the essence of the tree. One can find the existence of the seed in the roots, trunk, branches, leaves, flowers, and fruits. The tree cannot exist without the seed. Although it is not visible anymore, it exists in each cell of the tree. The connection of Mazda and creation is not like a painter and the painting, apart from each other. It is the relationship between a dancer and the dance. One cannot separate them from one another. The dance is a part of the dancer.

The human mind is the gate between the spirit world and the material world. The mind continues choosing between the two main spirits from the spirit world. If the mind is ignorant, the choices are based on desires and immediate gratification. It can cause pain and sorrow in our lives. Therefore, the mind needs to be guarded by consciousness, love, and wisdom to continue choosing good thoughts, good words, and good deeds. The ignorant mind chooses wicked thoughts, wicked words, and wicked deeds. Then, who we become depends on what mind we chose. As the result, we become either good or evil.

AHURA MAZDA
(The Supreme Wisdom)

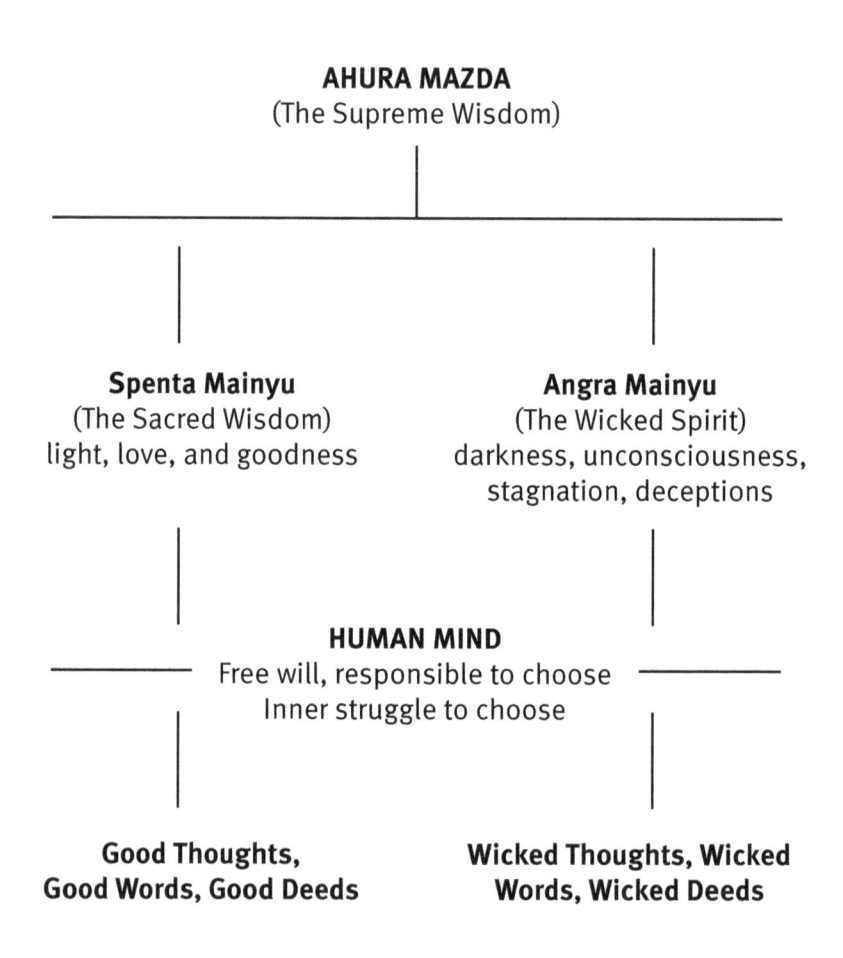

Spenta Mainyu
(The Sacred Wisdom)
light, love, and goodness

Angra Mainyu
(The Wicked Spirit)
darkness, unconsciousness,
stagnation, deceptions

HUMAN MIND
Free will, responsible to choose
Inner struggle to choose

**Good Thoughts,
Good Words, Good Deeds**

**Wicked Thoughts, Wicked
Words, Wicked Deeds**

Figure #1
These three levels are in our core being.
They are not outside us or separated from each other.

Zarathustra viewed humans as inherently good. However, though our lives are based on our circumstances, vulnerability, greed, and ignorance, we open our gates to the wicked spirits (mind). Therefore, he never condemned anyone, as it is not the person thinking, talking, and doing evil things. It is the negative spirits that we choose within us, gaining control of our mind. That is when the mob runs our lives. That is when the servants are running the kingdom in the absence of the king or the queen.

He does not condemn the angry person; he condemns the spirit of anger and of ignorance. That is why he called evil Angra Maiynu (Ahriman), The Angry Mind. If someone has the flu, it does not mean the person is bad. It is the flu virus that is the issue, not the person. If someone eats junk food every day and gets sick eventually, no one is punishing the individual except one's own actions. We cannot blame "God" or "Satan." We just need to look in the mirror.

> "By Thy perfect Intelligence, O Mazda, Thou didst first create us having bodies and spiritual consciences, and by Thy Thought gave ourselves the power of thought, word, and deed. Thus, leaving us free to choose our faith at our own will."
>
> (*Gathas:* Yasna 31.11)

As was mentioned before, we humans live in three worlds simultaneously. Being at those levels is not a physical. Rather, it is a mental and conscious state. In the physical level, we live in space and time. In the invisible world (soul and spirit), we live in a state of being. Mentally and emotionally, we all have different states. Are we calm or restless? Internally, we can only be aware of the state that we are. Similarly, in the invisible worlds (emotional, mental, and spiritual), we live in the state, not the space. The space can be measured physically such height, weight, length, etc. For instance, as a psychotherapist, one cannot measure a client's feelings physically. The feelings and thoughts do not have smell, weight, height, or colour to be measured. The measurement is in the state where the person is at.

The therapist asks the client, on the scale of 0–10, 0 to be very happy and 10 to be very sad, how sad they are feeling. Or, in the scale of 0–10, 0 to be very fearful and anxious and 10 to be very calm, how anxious they are. So, when we examine our internal world, one's state of consciousness determines the level of our being with the Good Spirit and Ahura Mazda. It is the degree and the state of our consciousness to The Higher Being that determines our connection.

1. *External/Material World* (*horizontal, linear, visible*) is experienced by our five senses. Most often we live and identify ourselves externally rather than being aware of our internal world. Who we think we are is often the identification with our external views of ourselves: career, gender, name, body size, physical appearance, or our social status. This is the world of space and time.

2. *Internal World* (*invisible, vertical, our state of being*)

A. Soul—our internal emotions and thoughts. The psychological work, how one thinks and feels, our state of being in the soul level—happy, sad, worried, think too much, how we interpret any events or judge people.

B. Spirit—our essence, true being, our "am-ness," *Fravashi*, our connection to the spirit world through consciousness, meditation, prayer, visions, or dreams. *"By Thy perfect*

Chapter 2 Free to Choose

Intelligence, O Mazda, Thou didst first create us having bodies and spiritual consciences."[15]

1. EXTERNAL, OUTER WORLD
Connect with the external world by our five senses

Smell   Sight   Sound

2. THE INNER WORLD

A. Soul: Emotion, Thoughts (psychological)

B. Spirit: Our True Being, Essence

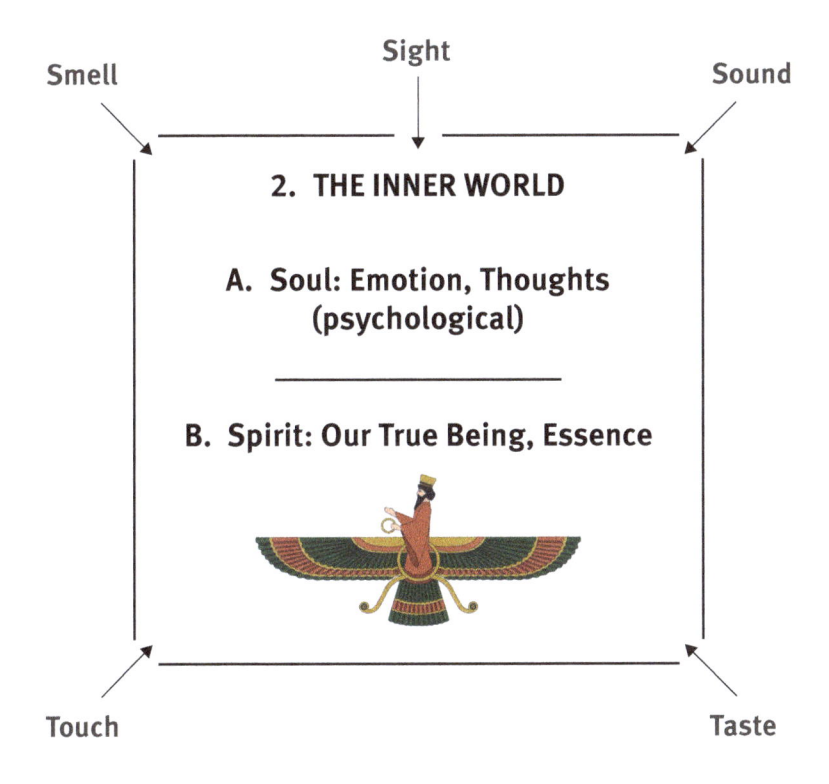

Touch   Taste

Figure #2

The inner and outer worlds in the human body.

---

15   Yasna 31.11

"Sin" Means Ignorance

> "Between these two Spirits the Demon-worshipers
> could not discern a right.
> To them Deception came at the time of decision,
> And they chose the Worst Mind.
> With violence then they rushed together,
> Life, in the world, to destroy."
>
> (*Gathas:* Yasna 30.6)

There are only two major sins in Zarathustra's point of view: ignorance and lack of love or goodness. All other sins such as hatred, violence, lies, jealousy, envy, and deceptions happen in the darkness of ignorance and lack of love. He is not there to condemn humanity for the sins that they commit. Instead, he encourages us to look at the inherent goodness within us and awaken our consciousness to a higher humanity. Only in the presence of wisdom and love is one immune from committing any sin or engaging in harmful thinking, hurtful words, and selfish actions. He is not there for condemnation, rather he is leading us toward a salvation of humanity from the prison of our darkness and ignorance and to becoming awakened individuals and conscious societies. Good and evil are unlimited paths. Either one is an ocean without a shore. There is no end to one's goodness, nor is there an end to one's wickedness. We humans are the gardeners of these seeds.

CHAPTER 3
You Are Responsible

Awakening Humanity's Choices and Responsibility

Zarathustra was ahead of his time and generation. His ideas were planted as seeds thousands of years ago to be harvested in our time.

> "May the people, O Lord of Life, give ear to a wise man whose teachings are soul heating and beneficial and act according to them in their lives."
>
> (*Gathas*: Yasna 31.19)

Everything in life grows effortlessly. Trees, animals, and almost every other being in the cosmos do not have the choice to develop themselves freely as they wish. Mostly, everything in the universe functions mechanically, based on instinct or on certain principles and laws. Existence develops and moves things naturally. Nature completes everything in the universe. A seed grows to become a flower without any effort. Earth moves around the sun naturally. Up to a certain point, nature oversees human development as well, both physically and biologically.

There is a part of human functioning that is beyond human effort. We don't need to consciously try to pump our heart—nature does it for us effortlessly. There is a part of our existence that functions instinctively. We don't digest our food, grow our hair or nails, breathe, filter what is not needed in our livers or kidneys, or circulate the blood in our veins.

Humans live in society. Another part of our growth develops within the limits imposed by family, school, culture, and religion. It takes great effort and conscious will to walk a different path or to think in different ways than the ones predetermined by society. With choice and consciousness also comes responsibility. In fact, the word "responsible" means the ability to respond (response-able). The ability to respond consciously and spontaneously to any circumstances in our lives.

Free to Act or to React

It is difficult to explore free choice without considering consciousness. Freedom has been mistakenly associated with chaos, selfishness, and anarchy, when one does not care about anybody but themselves. However, freedom does not mean being free to just do what one wants or fulfilling one's own desires without considering the consequences of one's actions. In contrast, freedom means to be responsible for one's thoughts, words, and actions. Only a conscious person is free: all other actions driven unconsciously bring more slavery, bondage, pain, hurt, and negative consequences. Reacting instead of responding means to act unconsciously.

Chapter 3 You Are Responsible

An unconscious person is doomed to react. In fact, most of our assumed free choices are little but reactions to our past conditioning. Reactive behaviour seems to be the norm. When someone taps you on the knee, you are not free to keep your leg still. Your body simply reacts to the stimulus and moves. When someone insults us, we react similarly, being triggered unconsciously. Likewise, reaction is our slavery to our past conditioning and experiences. A conscious person, however, does not automatically react to stimulus, but rather responds to the immediate circumstances guided by wisdom, awareness, and choice. Such actions are immediate and driven by one's awareness. A Zen master once said: *"No one can insult me, since I don't ask for respect."*

> "So may we be like those making the world progress toward perfection; May Mazda and the Divine Spirits help us and guide our efforts through Truth; For a thinking man [conscious person] is where Wisdom is at home."
>
> (*Gathas*: Yasna 30.9)

The choice we have is like holding a knife. We can use it to stab someone or to hurt ourselves, to peel a potato or give it to a sculptor to create a beautiful statue. It all depends in whose hand that knife is and what we do with it. If our choices are in accordance with goodness and wisdom, we become the master, and one with Mazda. If not, we live like slaves to the forces of darkness and ignorance. If someone drops a hammer on their feet, no one punishes the person. The pain is the result of one's action, not God's punishment.

> "Zarathustra brings a total revolution in the concept of God and religion. Now religion is no longer a worship or a belief; now religion becomes the greatest creative act of man."
>
> (*Zarathustra: The Laughing Prophet* by Osho)

Fravashi: The Symbol—The Authentic Self

There is a part of Mazda in us that is called *Fravashi* (our essence, true self). It is our spirit, which has pre-existed this life and will survive after death. Our essence *(Fravashi)* is considered holy, who existed from the dawn of time before the beginning of creation. It is a human with two wings. *Fravashi* is the symbol of Zoroastrianism. This symbol represents the authentic self, the real self, or the divine self.

Within each person, there are two kinds of selves. One is our personality and the other is the authentic self, or *Fravashi*. Personality comes from the word *persona* meaning *mask* in Greek. The *persona* is the mask that we wear based on our culture, society, age, gender, circumstances, and social class. As

Chapter 3   You Are Responsible

we grow, different events, circumstances, and people influence our personalities.

Most often, we connect with our persona like, "*I am a kind person,*" "*I am a dentist,*" "*I am a man or a woman.*" When we are not conscious, we relate to our personality. And there is a crowd in the personality. We can have thousands of "i's" and identities inside. We live our lives based on our imagination of who we are. We also have a concept of who others are. As long as we perceive ourselves based on our imagination, we never see our true self or that of others.

However, there is only one true self within that is not earthly – the real "I", not false "i"s. It is the spirit of the divine Ahura Mazda. It is immortal. When we are in touch with the real self, we are authentic. "*I am that I am.*" When we relate to our identities and persona, we shift continuously from oneself to another. We are in chaos. This is a major issue in a human psychic and dysfunction when one is not in touch with the permanent self (*Fravashi*).

This symbol represents the authentic self, the real self, or the divine self. Most often we are unconscious and not in touch with the authentic self (*Fravashi*). We are so preoccupied with our personality, day to day affairs, struggles, pains, and distractions that pull us outside ourselves and make us neglect connecting to the real self. The busier we are, the less connected we become to our essence.

We are born with essence, the authentic self (*Fravashi*), but it is latent like a seed until it is cultivated and matures. In a spiritual sense, as far as we connect to our personality, we live in our earthly life. We also need to remember that we have a spiritual life as well. One cannot go to the spiritual life through the personality because our personalities only function in a society. If you are alone in the forest, do you really have a personality to show to anyone? In our day-to-day life, we go out, have a name, and a profession. We function through our personality with others.

It is like wearing clothes to go outside. We put on boots, a parka, shawl, and hat to cover ourselves. But we know deep inside that those clothes are not us. When we come back home and take off our clothes, who we are becomes more evident and visible. Similarly, *Fravashi*, the real authentic part of us, is hidden. The real self is covered by the clothes and dresses of our personality. To go to the divine level and to know Ahura Mazda, we must awaken *Fravashi*, the real self.

The apple seed cannot become an apple tree unless we plant the seed in the soil. Then, we water it and look after it. It takes effort and work to grow the seed to become an apple tree. Eventually, when the tree grows fully, it gives the fruit of the apples. But this growth and process do not happen unless the seed is cultivated. Similarly, we need to cultivate the seed of *Fravashi* in the soil of our consciousness. We need to continuously witness and look after it in our thoughts, words, and deeds to evolve it fully to become "Mazda-like."

Our authentic self is like a dimmer. It starts from a dark and low point until we keep increasing the brightness of it to lighten our space fully. Through the authentic self, our consciousness increases and becomes more receptive to the love and wisdom of Mazda. Therefore, in our spiritual growth, the most important aspect of our work is to be receptive and open

Chapter 3   You Are Responsible

to Mazda internally. Surrendering is a crucial matter in every spiritual growth. However, Zarathustra encourages people to surrender themselves not to a particular person or ideas, but rather to divine love and consciousness.

> "I am not this hair,
> I am not this skin,
> I am the soul that lives within."
>
> Rumi

The Symbol of *Fravashi*

Figure #3

Fravashi: the immortal self within.

The symbol of Zoroastrianism is a human with wings like an eagle, able to fly to our ultimate being. In the symbol:

1. Wisdom of Age: The face is an elderly human who has gained wisdom, looking forward to growth and freedom, and turning away from ignorance.

2. Three Principles of Zarathustra: The upper wings have three layers representing the three principles of Zarathustra: good thoughts, good words, and good deeds.

3. Three Opposing Forces: The lower part of the symbol (like an upper tail) also consists of three separate parts. The tail represents wicked thoughts, wicked words, and wicked deeds. If they are chosen in a wrong path, it can bring misfortune and misery to a human's life. That is why they are in the lower part of the symbol—our animalistic part.

4. Positive and Negative Forces: There are two loops at the two sides of *Fravashi*, which are representative of positive forces (The Sacred Wisdom—*Spenta Mainyu*) and negative forces (Wicked Force—*Ahriman, Satan, Angra Mainyu*). The positive loop is directed in front of the face, meaning to proceed forward toward goodness. The negative loop is located at the back, meaning to turn away from wickedness.

5. Our Spirit Is Immortal, Eternity in Universe: The central circle around *Fravashi's* trunk symbolizes that the spirit is immortal, similar to a circle having neither a beginning nor an end.

6. Choosing the Right Path: One of the old man's hands is pointing upward, indicating that human beings need to struggle to grow toward their full potential.

7. Path of Loyalty and Faithfulness: On the other hand, there is a ring, similar to a ring of promise representing a wedding ceremony. It is a ring of covenant for one's promise for faithfulness and loyalty in the path toward goodness and wisdom.

Gender Equality

One of the fundamental teachings of Zarathustra is that Mazda has granted us free will, and every individual, regardless of their gender or ethnic background, needs to make his or her own choices. Slavery was highly forbidden under Persian empires and Zoroastrianism. No one had the right to take freedom from anyone else. Men also were not allowed to reduce women to an unequal status. Both men and women were equally permitted to make their own choices, leading to right thinking and right actions.

Zarathustra viewed Mazda as the personified Divine Wisdom, which existed as a seed within each human being. In contrast to God as a male, *Ahura Mazda* is neither masculine nor feminine. It is both and neither. In Persian language, *Ahura* (Lord) is masculine, and *Mazda* (Wisdom) is feminine. In Zarathustra's point of view, femininity has the spirit of wisdom (*Mazda*). It is a life force and often associated with water, and the moon (*Anahita*, or *Nahid* ناهید, feminine source in ancient Persia). Masculinity is associated with light, consciousness, having a sense of purpose and direction in life, and the material world (*Mithra,* masculine source in ancient Persia).

Feminine force (*Mazda*) is a force that brings life to a matter. Without a form (*Ahura*) also, life cannot manifest itself. A flower needs a pot to hold it to grow. A plant cannot grow without a container, and a container without a plant growing in it is dead. Both masculine and feminine are interdependent on one another, not in opposition, similar to *Ahura Mazda*. Existence is like a river: feminine symbolically is like water flowing in the river, and masculine is similar to a riverbed, creating a container for the river to flow. They are interdependent and need one another. A masculine energy needs to work on his consciousness, grounding, stability, and be a container. A feminine energy needs to work on her nourishing, wisdom, and aliveness. Both forces exist in each human being (*Ahura Mazda,* masculine and feminine). This concept was later developed further after Zarathustra to Tantra (*Shiva* and *Shakti*) and in Taoism (*Yin* and *Yang*).

Even the words *Ahura Mazda* have equality in both masculine and feminine roots. It is important to point out that masculine and feminine does not mean men and women only. Men and women have both attributes within. A man can be more feminine than a woman; similarly, a woman can have more masculine attributes than a man. Feminine and masculine in Zarathustra also mean the spirits and the energy of both that exist within each of us and in the universe. According to Zarathustra, Mazda (the feminine aspect) plays a significant part in existence. Although the women's right movement is very recent in the West, women in no other society have been known to have such independence and gender equality than 2,500 years ago in Persian Zoroastrian society. Throughout the *Gathas*, Zarathustra particularly emphasized the importance of both men and women's partnership in bringing goodness, light, and wisdom into the world.

The Greeks and Romans often portrayed Persian men as dominated by their women and ridiculed them as weak and "unmanly" as compared with themselves. This was an excellent example of the importance of the status of women in Zoroastrian culture. Women held positions as government officials, supervisors, soldiers, army commanders, and even queens. Zoroastrian women could reach the highest religious position. Girls could not be forced into a marriage without their consent. Zarathustra addressed his own younger daughter in the *Gathas* regarding her marriage to find a partner based on her own choice.

> Mazda Ahura has bestowed upon you as husband and Lord, the person who has deep attachment to Vohuman [Good Mind] and Truth. Therefore, consult with your inner self and wisdom, and act through Armaiti [the spirit of devotion and faith].
>
> (*Gathas*: Yasna 53.3)

In the *Gathas,* Zarathustra treats both men and women alike, and often addresses them equally when speaking to human beings.

"Listen with your ears the highest truth, consider them with illumined minds carefully and decide each man and woman personally between the two paths, good and evil."

(*Gathas*: Yasna 30.2)

"The man or woman who performs the work which has been declared as the best by Thee, O Ahura Mazda."

(*Gathas*: Yasna 46.10)

One needs to realize that he spoke about five thousand years ago, when women were extremely oppressed in every society. We are still struggling with this issue at the present time. It needs to be reminded that women did not have the right to vote until 1920 in the United States. Still to date, many women are not being treated equally to men under constitutional laws in some countries. In fact, many consider Zarathustra to be the initiator of the idea of women's rights and gender equality.

CHAPTER 4
The Purpose of Human Life

Wisdom Is Not Knowledge

There is a pre-existing wisdom behind the principles that guide everything that maintains structure, harmony, and balance in the universe. Zarathustra names the harmony and wisdom behind existence as *Asha* (*Artha*—art in English meaning harmony and balance).

> *"In accord with the everlasting Law of Asha or Truth, which forms fundamentals of life, everyone should act."*
> (*Gathas*: Yasna 33.1)

This force to grow and to evolve happens in two directions: horizontally and vertically. On a horizontal level, one needs to grow from being a child to an adolescent, to a young adult, to go to school, choose a career, marry, have children, accomplish things in life, and so on. The horizontal level is about surviving, reproduction, adapting, accumulating wealth and knowledge, and progressing in life. The horizontal level is about one's accomplishment in life externally, from birth to death. It is a linear line from past to present and into the future.

The inner growth, however, can be pictured on a vertical level. It is the growth of wisdom, love, and consciousness from a lower and animalistic level to the higher and godly level. Wisdom is, of course, very different from knowledge. Wisdom belongs to this higher level of existence. It is on a vertical and a spiritual level. Wisdom is life experience, to know good from bad, and right from wrong.

Vertical Level
(higher consciousness, wisdom, eternity)

↑

| Past | Present | Future → |

Horizontal, Linear Direction

↓

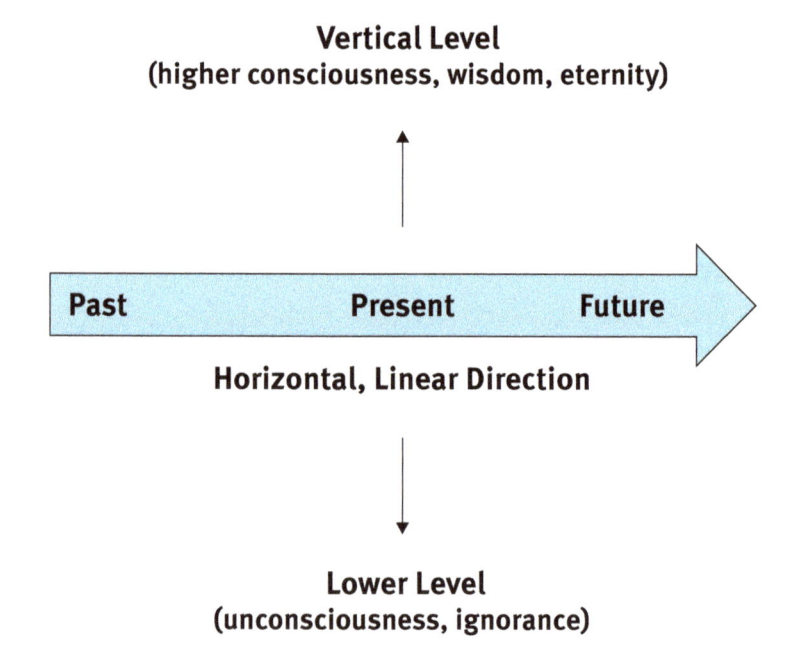

Lower Level
(unconsciousness, ignorance)

Figure #4
The vertical and horizontal directions in a human's life.

According to Zarathustra, "good" is an unselfish choice that one makes consciously that is beneficial not only to the self but also in consideration of other beings as well. "Righteousness" does not mean following certain rituals or morality blindly. Rather, it means living a life of respect and dignity for the self and other beings and choosing the right path. Good is a compassionate and humanitarian choice that one makes wisely toward the self and others. Righteousness means to follow the right path that is respectful to the well-being of all.

Consciousness and Mind: "Seeing" Is Not "Thinking"

Consciousness is the ability to see things truly, like in a mirror, without fabricating them. Mind is the interpretation of a phenomena, while consciousness is seeing what it is as is. In Eastern spirituality, the function of consciousness is to see, and the function of the mind is to think. You don't need to think about whether you are reading this book. You already know because you are aware of it. You don't need anyone's proof to know what space you are in. You already know it consciously, and you don't need anyone's approval or acknowledgement. However, in our mind, we think; we don't know. We can think and plan our schedule for the next day, but we do not know for sure what tomorrow will bring. If we are conscious, we all see the same thing. Consciousness brings oneness and unity. However, the mind divides us since there are many minds interpreting and idealizing what one sees. The interpretation of what one sees is the function of the mind. A Higher Being is the same, but every religion, philosopher, or ideology describes it differently.

Mind means conditioning and the penetration of a truth within us. Consciousness is one, whereas mind is many. We can have a man or a woman's mind, a Buddhist or a Christian mind, and a logical or a superstitious mind. However, we cannot have a logical or an engineer consciousness. There are so many minds because there are many religions, ideas, philosophies, educations, and cultures. Everyone does not have a single mind. We all have many minds depending on the circumstances. The mind is a part of our brain function that assists us in categorizing, memorizing, thinking, naming, and problem-solving. When we park a car in a parking lot, the mind helps us to remember where it is parked. It also helps us not to take someone else's car. The mind is there to serve us in life. However, in most cases, we become the slave to the mind and how it sees things, rather than making the mind serve us.

The mind often becomes an obstacle. It blocks us from seeing things from the eye of consciousness. It becomes like a dark cloud covering the light of consciousness. Unless one does not examine the nature of his or her mind and dissolve it, one cannot go deeper within or see the truth as it is. Hopefully, there comes a time in our lives when we begin questioning what has been indoctrinated in us by our environment. In Zen, it is called "to find out our original face." The essence that we were all born with.

According to Zarathustra, our mind and heart are like gates. Similar to any country's borders that check who can enter a country and who can't, we also need to guard our minds and hearts in order to be protected from any dark spirits entering into our beings. It is better to guard our mind and heart at the beginning from those dark spirits such as addiction, anxiety, depression, aggression, or hate. We need to protect ourselves and deal with them when they are already within us rather than being caught later with negativity if we are neglectful at first.

Chapter 4 The Purpose of Human Life

In some spiritual practices, love is important and in others it may be consciousness. However, in Zarathustra's teachings, love and consciousness are twin spirits. Love without wisdom can be naïve. And consciousness without love can lead to selfishness or egoism. Love gives life to consciousness and consciousness gives eyes to love to see. We become like a bird with two wings, having both love and wisdom connected to us.

The mind is like a child that seeks pleasure and immediate gratification. If the mind is not guarded by consciousness, it could make harmful choices. Similarly, a parent does not leave a child alone in a rough neighbourhood to play alone in the playground. The parent may sit on the bench and watch the child to not get hurt by anyone or their self. Consciousness also needs to watch the mind in the playground of life in order not to allow a harmful spirit to fool the mind.

There is a story about two beggars. One was blind, and the other crippled. Once, there was a fire in the building where they both stayed. The crippled beggar could not run, and the blind person could not see where to escape. So, the crippled beggar sat on the shoulders of the blind one, directing the blind one where to go and to escape. The teamwork and the balance created between them allowed them to escape. Similarly, consciousness can see but it cannot walk on Earth, since it is from a higher level of existence. The mind is the blind one who can walk on Earth but does not have the wisdom to see where to go. The balance and harmony between them, according to Zarathustra, is called a state of happiness (Asha).

> "One who makes his mind better or worse, O Mazda, his deed, word and conscience shall follow sure. The path selected by one's voluntary choice, his will and faith shall also follow the same and shall be in tune with them. According to Thy wisdom, O Mazda, their destiny shall be distinct from each other."
>
> (*Gathas*: Yasna 48.4)

Happiness Is Not a State of Comfort

> "In humble adoration, with hands outstretched I pray to Thee, O Mazda! First of all, through Thy Holy spirit vouchsafe to me All righteousness of action, all wisdom of the Good Mind, That I may thereby bring joy to the Soul of Creation."
>
> (*Gathas*: Yasna 28.1)

Happiness cannot be achieved by accumulating things, mindless entertainment, or by selfishly looking after number one—me. Zarathustra teaches that joyfulness and peacefulness can only be achieved in relation to other people's happiness, the care of animals, and of every living creature on Earth. He often speaks of two worlds, the physical (visible, material) and metaphysical (invisible, spiritual, consciousness). These two worlds are interrelated. Human beings live and move between these two worlds simultaneously. The work of a man or a woman is to live in union with these two worlds consciously, joyfully, and harmoniously. Disharmony between these two worlds creates illness and suffering in one's life.

> *"Mazda Ahura, the Absolute Ruler, has specified that good fortune is for him who makes others happy."*
>
> (*Gathas*: Yasna 43.1)

We may define happiness as when we are not sad. What kind of happiness is that? Most often we don't know how to be happy because we are happy. We feel happy when we are not in pain. We mistakenly confuse pleasure with happiness. For many, happiness means just to be comfortable. Comfort is very different from happiness. In fact, too much comfort can create dullness, laziness, and stagnation. Zarathustra calls this state *Ahriman* (evil in English)—a state of stagnation and vegetation. Or one may call it "too much comfort."

Our basic needs must be met to be comfortable, to do our work, and to grow. However, we cannot just live in comfort without being challenged in life. There should be safety in order to dare to be unsafe. But safety alone does not bring us happiness, otherwise the only safe place would be the grave, and the only comfortable people would be dead people. They are all resting comfortably in peace. Yes, a dead person is comfortable in the coffin without worrying about the news, paying the bills, going to work, or arguing with their spouse. They are all comfortable resting in peace, but they are rotting within.

Only an alive person, full of life, can feel happiness since that person is taking the risk to be fully alive. Zarathustra calls this state of aliveness *"inner fire."* And, without the insecurity of risk, there is no possibility of real life. Zarathustra describes maintaining this balance as a *Chinvat Bridge*. It is a bridge that separates the world of the living from the world of the dead. Life is like walking on a rope (*Chivant Bridge*), similar to a tightrope walker. We always must maintain our balance in life (*Asha*—harmony). Otherwise, we fall from the bridge like a tightrope walker.

Do you know that we are always walking on the *Chivant Bridge* every second of our life, tightrope walkers between life and death? Do you know that it is possible that you will not be alive in the next hour? How do you know when you go to sleep that it will not be the last time you are alive? We go on in life assuming we are here forever and take life for granted. We have lots of time to kill. There is a saying in English, *"killing time."* Don't you think that is a deception? We don't kill time. Time is killing us. We waste much of our lives on unimportant things, getting entangled with so many distractions that we never live our lives fully. So, we had best wake up to a fundamental reality: One never knows when he or she may fall from the *Chivant Bridge*. So, walk on it with consequences and awareness, like a tightrope walker, as Zarathustra points out.

Happiness comes in the balance of safety and unsafety, like the pedals of a bicycle. When one is down, the other is up. They cannot be at the same place at the same time. They are not opposite. They are in pairs (twin spirits). The balance of both going up and down makes the bicycle move, like a pendulum of a clock. True happiness means peace, harmony, and balance, not only for the individual person, but also for the happiness of others.

This peace is only possible when we are in harmony within our bodies, emotions, and thoughts. It is only when one has transcended the inner tension and conflict and come to a calm state that one can find true peace. A peaceful person is one who is not in conflict within themselves. Peace is possible when one is governed by wisdom and goodness. Happiness is not egotistical. Only by sharing this peaceful, balanced state are we then capable of acting as loving and kind people to others and to Earth. A person who lives in chaos and anarchy within themselves cannot bring peace to others, nor be truly happy themselves. True happiness is achieved when one's thoughts, words, and deeds are guided by wisdom and goodness.

Asha (Harmony and Balance): Both Internally and Externally

> Zarathustra, amongst all the religious founders, is the only one who is life-affirmative, who is not against life, whose religion is a religion of celebration, of gratefulness to existence. He is not against the pleasures of life, and he is not in favor of renouncing the world. On the contrary, he is in absolute support of rejoicing in the world, because except for this life and this world, all are hypothetical ideologies. God, heaven and hell, they are all projections of the human mind, not authentic experiences; they are not realities. Zarathustra is unique. He is the only one who is not against life, who is for life; whose god is not somewhere else; whose god is

nothing but another name for life itself. And to live totally, to live joyously and to live intensely, is all that religion is based on.

(Zarathustra: A God that Can Dance by Osho)

The main purpose of our existence in life is to grow from ignorance to wisdom, to do our inner work, and to gain wisdom like Mazda (good thoughts, good words, and good deeds). We are also not just here to have a selfish life. Rather, we are here to help other human beings in their inner and outer growth in life. At the same time, we are to look after all other beings in existence and to be protective of Earth wisely, as it is in heaven. That is why gardening in most ancient Zoroastrian's homes was important as a reminder and symbol of Heaven on Earth.

Zarathustra is known as the first environmentalist, who advocated a lot for the well-being of Earth. It is a responsibility of each Zoroastrian to protect air, earth, fire, and water.

> "Unto you, O Creator, the Soul of Mother Earth complained thus: Wherefore did you create me? Who gave life to me? Anger, rapine, outrage, blunder, aggression and violence are everywhere. There is no protector for me, except Thee. Therefore, reveal to me a savior who could show me a way out of this difficulty."
>
> (*Gathas*: Yasna 29.1)

Chapter 4   The Purpose of Human Life

"O Ahura Mazda, and O Spirit of Truth and Right! Do Ye grant me and my followers such authority and power through Truth, that with the Good Mind, we may bring the world peace and happiness, Of which, Thou, O Lord, art indeed the first possessor."

(*Gathas*: Yasna 29.10

He believed that we are here on Earth to grow and be wise and to have a happy and joyful life. The purpose of our lives is to make Earth like a paradise. We are not here to suffer but to be happy.

CHAPTER 5
The Inner Alchemy

Mazdaism—The Followers of Wisdom

Mazdaism's teachings are an inner work, based on oral tradition. The wisdom has been transmitted orally through centuries from the time of Zarathustra. The magi, who were the closest ones in Zarathustra's inner circle, learned directly from him. Later, they passed the wisdom to others through the oral tradition. He declared that "God— Mazda" is only one and is the source of holy intelligence and wisdom. Subsequently, we humans possess intelligence and consciousness similar to Mazda when we connect and expand this holy treasure within us. He encouraged us to achieve "Mazda-hood" through self-realization (*Haurvatat*—perfection, realization) and self-purification.

> "The two gifts of perfection and eternity, O my Lord,
> shall lead the people to spiritual and inner light."
>
> (*Gathas*: Yasna 34.11)

While spiritual work is based on esoteric teachings and is an inner transformation of a lower to a higher self and consciousness, religion is about the outer work (exoteric aspects) and is concerned about human external affairs in life.

"Exoteric derives from Latin exotericus, which is itself from Greek exōterikos, meaning 'external,' and ultimately from exō, meaning 'outside.' Exō has a number of offspring in English, including exotic, exonerate, exorbitant, and the combining form exo- or ex- (as in exoskeleton and exobiology). The antonym of exoteric is esoteric, meaning 'designed for or understood by the specially initiated alone'; it descends from the Greek word for 'within,' esō."[16]

Religion is based on external ethical codes in order to keep humanity together within a certain pre-set guidance. Zarathustra's concern was not to give people any commandments but to extend their consciousness to choose based on their own wisdom.

A Few Principles of Mazdaism

The focus of the Mazdaism teachings is based on a few principles:

Focus on Oral Tradition: As metal cannot transform to gold by itself and needs the wisdom of the alchemist, human transformation cannot be gained by reading books or working alone in isolation. One needs a school, a teacher, and teaching by those who have already grown consciously (the magi).

---

16 "Exoteric" definition and meaning, *The Merriam-Webster Dictionary*, https://www.merriam-webster.com/dictionary/exoteric.

Self-Remembering: To begin with our inner growth, we need to admit that we are not conscious human beings yet. Self-remembering means to remember ourselves as who we really are (our essence "I," not personality "i"s) and to move from an unconsciousness to a conscious person. This transformation is the purpose of all human beings.

There is a difference between honesty and sincerity. Honesty means when one is being truthful to others. Sincerity is when one is being truthful to oneself. Humans are "lying animals." The good thoughts and good words mantra of Zarathustra means to be sincere to ourselves. We lie constantly to ourselves. In psychotherapy, it is called a self-defence mechanism. Our psyches continuously justify, rationalize, deny, react, repress, or project our reality in order to deal with our unpleasant circumstances.

Self-remembering or having a "good thought" means to be aware of our lies and to see things naturally as they are without any fabrication of reality. When we are conscious of our own inner lies, we speak good (good words) internally, and subsequently externally. Zarathustra teaches us that to see the truth and the good begins with the ability to see first behind our inner lies. Otherwise, we could be honest people but insincere within. To be sincere means to be authentic.

Humanity Is Fundamentally Good, Not Evil: We are all born good and innocent. Depending on our circumstances, we can be damaged, hurt, corrupted, or wicked in our lives. Like a potato, when it is not cultivated in the soil, the roots grow very crooked in a dark space. The negative parts of us are like the crooked roots in a potato. Similarly, when we do not grow in a healthy environment, negativity grows in the dark. But those negatives are not us. They are negative spirits that have been in us, such as depression, anger, violence, greed, anxiety, or addictions. These are the spirits we pick through our lives. This is not who we are. As we drive a car in the mud and get dirty, we also pick up negative spirits (energy) in our souls.

Like the snake shedding its old skin, we also need to get rid of those negative spirits (energy) in order to let the healthier characters grow. We choose to be born to our original goodness. This time, we select our new skin and characters with consciousness and with love. Through increasing our consciousness, we humans also can fly like an eagle to reach the sky of Ahura Mazda. The Divine within us is the origin of who we truly are. We begin to know that we may appear to be separated in the body, but we are one and united in essence.

> "In fact, my soul and yours are the same. You appear in me, and I appear in you. We hide in each other."
>
> (Rumi)

Conscience (*Daenâ*): The central aim of Zarathustra's guidance is the development of conscience or *Daenâ*. Religion according to him is not external, rather it is internal. He called it *Daenâ* (conscience). *Daenâ* (*Din*) means religion. It means *Didan* in Persian (to see). It means to perceive to conceive. It is based on a person's inner perception to "see."

Our Higher Being: Metaphorically, we touch the ground with our earthly and physical feet and our head is up toward the sky, our higher being. We connect to the external world physically by our five senses and connect with our higher being within through our spirit (consciousness).

To realize the true self, we need to create a division between the observer (seer) and the subject of the observation (seen). The observer within us is our higher being. It is Mazda within us. The observer is our essence, the real "I." Unless we divide ourselves into two, we cannot grow from our animalistic part of the self (the lower) to the higher one. This division is called "inner separation." The Mazdaism work taught by Zarathustra is the inner alchemy to awaken the observer within us to the degree that we are fully present, when transformed from the lower part into Ahura Mazda.

There was once a mystic near death. His students asked him for his last advice before he died. He said, "Swim, but don't get wet." What he meant was to live your life but don't identify with your circumstances. Human beings are like a circle. There is a centre in us (essence) and the circumference (events). Our centre (essence) always remains the same, but people or events come and go around our centre in the circumference. From when we get up in the morning until we go to sleep, from birth to death, we are always there at the centre despite of our circumstances. The esoteric teaching is not about changing the self from outside of us. It is about a shift in our inner consciousness and being within us. This inner transformation is the Eastern spirituality and psychology.

Conclusion

Zarathustra's teachings and philosophy have been diffused and developed into many cultures and belief systems worldwide throughout history. According to his view, there are two spirits in a human's mind from which to choose: the spirit of Sacred Wisdom or progressive and wickedness or stagnation. We are gifted with the power of choice and consciousness to walk our paths in life based on the choices we make. Religion based on Zarathustra's point of view needs to be a living force like a fire within every human being—to walk life like a tightrope walker and determine our destiny continuously. This is a moral choice driven from one's conscience (*Daena*) and should not be confined by reading scriptural texts.

There is one Supreme Being that is The Essence of existence—Ahura Mazda (the source of wisdom and consciousness). Like H2O is the source of water, or a seed is in the core of a tree and its branches and fruits, Mazda is not apart from us, but rather within the existence of all beings. Mazda is the source of goodness, love, and wisdom, not the source of fear, revenge, punishment, or jealousy. We are not here to be fearful of this source, but rather to be friends and coworkers of Mazda in life toward a higher existence and becoming conscious beings.

As the flame of any fire moves upward, human beings should improve themselves in order to progress in life. In Zarathustra's point of view, the relationship between Ahura Mazda and humans is not a relationship of a child to a parent, nor a slave to a master. He views human beings as friends and coworkers of Ahura Mazda. We are given free choice and the intelligence to be responsible for our choices in order to choose wisdom, like a flame moving upward toward the Higher Being. There is a co-relationship between us.

> *"O, Lord of Life and Wisdom, I desire a vision of Thee and communion with Thee as a friend."*
>
> (*Gathas*: Yasna 33.6)

When we look at ourselves, we realize that we are not really who we have chosen to be so far. Nobody chooses to be who they are. It just happens gradually through our family, culture, religion, gender, or age. We keep picking things up, like a camel, without questioning what we are loading ourselves up with. As children, we are vulnerable. We come into life innocent, good, and pure, not evil. Then, we all get polluted, contaminated by our environment.

This journey of awareness is only possible for humans. Our destiny is to complete ourselves on Earth. We are not yet fully human. We are travelling on a bridge from being an animal to becoming a human in the full sense of the word. In Zarathustra's view, this journey is to assist humanity to cross the bridge and to evolve into decent, loving, wise, and conscious human beings. As you look at our world today, you will agree that we are desperately in need of this quality of humanity.

Conclusion

We humans are born to be the master of our destiny. However, this mastery is not given to us freely. We need to work for it. One cannot be a pilot without working hard. One needs to put his or her full effort into it because that's our true achievement in life. It is good to have a job. It is good to have a home. It is good to have a family. But all these will be gone one day. They are all impermanent. What is permanent? It is what is in us—the kingdom of heaven, *Fravashi*, the spirit of Mazda within us. The spirit (*Fravashi*) that never dies and never was born, that does not have a beginning nor an end. It is *alpha*, and it is *omega*.

Although humans have the highest level of consciousness on Earth, we have not finished and completed our full conscious potential yet. We still have a long way to go in our process toward perfection. Our existence has a purpose from birth to death: to complete ourselves from a lower to a higher being, to make the earth like a paradise, and to reach to the higher level of wisdom and consciousness toward Mazda-hood. Humans are not born to creep and to crawl on Earth like caterpillars. We are born to transform into butterflies, into an enlightened and conscious human being—to become "the one who possesses the Golden Light."

A Butterfly Poem by G. Eustace Owen

A butterfly rested upon a flower,
Gay was he and light as a flake,
And there he met a caterpillar
Sobbing as though his heart would break;
It hurt the happy butterfly

Born to Fly

To see a caterpillar cry.

Said he, "Whatever is the matter?
And may I
help you in any way?"
"I've lost my brother," wept the other,
"He has been unwell for many a day;
Now I discover, sad to tell,
He's only a dead and empty shell."

"Unhappy grub, be done with weeping,
Your sickly brother is not dead:
His body's stronger and no longer
Crawls like a worm but flies instead. He dances through
the sunny hours
And drinks sweet nectar from the flowers."

"Away, away deceitful villain,
Go to the winds where you belong.
I won't be grieving at your leaving,
So, take away your lying tongue.
Am I a foolish slug or snail,
To swallow such a fairy tale?"

"I'll prove my words, you unbeliever,
Now listen well, and look at me.
I am none other than your brother,
Alive and well and fancy free.
Soon you'll be with me in the skies
Among the flirting butterflies."

**MAY THE SPIRIT OF LOVE
AND WISDOM OF**

MAZDA BE ALWAYS OUR GUIDE

www.zarathustra.ca